W9-BVF-708

STEP-BY-STEP GUIDE TO GROWING BONSAI TREES

STEP-BY-STEP GUIDE TO GROWING BONSAI TREES

Joan Melville

PHOTOGRAPHS BY GRAEME

LINE DRAWINGS BY THE AUTHOR

PELHAM BOOKS

First published in Great Britain by Pelham Books Ltd
52 Bedford Square, London, W.C.1
1973

ISBN 0 7207 0672 6

Set and printed in Great Britain by
Tonbridge Printers Ltd, Tonbridge, Kent
in Baskerville eleven on fourteen point
on paper supplied by P. F. Bingham Ltd,
and bound by James Burn at Esher, Surrey

Acknowledgements

My thanks to A. E. M. Jansen for making this book possible; to Eleanor Due-Lund, who kindly typed the manuscript; and to Mrs Young, of Bromage and Young, who kindly allowed her many beautiful trees to be photographed.

Joan Melville
Red Leaf Cottage,
Richmond,
Surrey

Contents

Illustrations

PHOTOGRAPHS

LINE DRAWINGS

INTRODUCTION

My interest in miniature trees dates back to my girlhood, when I lived in what was then known as India, but is now part of Pakistan. In the vestibule of a hotel in Karachi, I saw palms growing in quite small tubs and I wondered how it was possible for such ultimately large plants to grow in so small a space. On approaching the gardener, I was told that the tap-root was cut off at an early stage, leaving the fibrous roots to thicken up. It was this treatment that limited the size of the plant. The gardener also told me that the plant was fed with a manure compost and with other ingredients the nature of which I could not glean from him. The plants lived for many years in this confined space. Each morning the gardener would lovingly wash down the leaves and clear up any bits and pieces thrown into the tub. He only became really annoyed when guests threw their lighted cigarette butts into the tub. His language in his own dialect, some of which I could understand, would have made the miscreants' ears burn.

Although the palms were too large for the average household, my interest was aroused and I sought for more knowledge. By a stroke of luck, I met a Japanese family residing in India who had brought several bonsai trees from Japan; the trees had been passed down to the son, who in his turn would pass them on to his eldest son. The family taught me a great deal and had infinite patience with my initial blunders.

Bonsai literally means 'planted in a small tray or pot'. The Japanese art of bonsai has been passed on from generation to generation. Some of the trees are worth a bounty; yet, for many families, these little gems are beauty beyond price, taking a place of honour in their homes. My Japanese friends told me that in Tokyo the temperature rarely falls below 37°F. in the coldest month of January, rising each morning to around 78°F. in the hottest month of August, and dropping to 41°F. in December, with humidity little below 62. These conditions are ideal for bonsai trees.

During my years in Malta I came across citrus fruit-trees growing in pots to decorate balconies and terraces. Here again, I learnt that the pruning of the roots enabled the trees to live in small pots. By observing oranges, grapefruit, figs and peaches grown in this way, I acquired some useful knowledge for later years.

Many moons were to pass before I found myself in a position to make practical use of the lessons I had learnt. My first garden in Britain was used as a teaching area in horticulture and garden design, until circumstances forced me to move to a flat in London. It was not until a few years ago that I at last found the time to start growing miniature trees by the bonsai method.

Richmond Park is within easy distance from where I now live. In this beautiful natural park I came to realize how magnificent our British trees are – the oak, elm, chestnut and

---

Fig. 1a: 1 Horse Chestnut (*Aesculus*) white flower; 1a Horse Chestnut, red flower; 2 Hornbeam (*Carpinus*); 3 Alder (*Alnus*); 3a *Alnus incisa*, not often seen today; 4 Ash (*Fraxinus*); 5 Beech (*Fagus*); 5a Beech, cut leaf variety; 6 Birch (*Betula*) male; 6a Birch, female; 7 Sweet chestnut (*Castanea*); 8 Common Maple (*Acer*); 9 Sycamore (*Acer pseudoplatanus*)

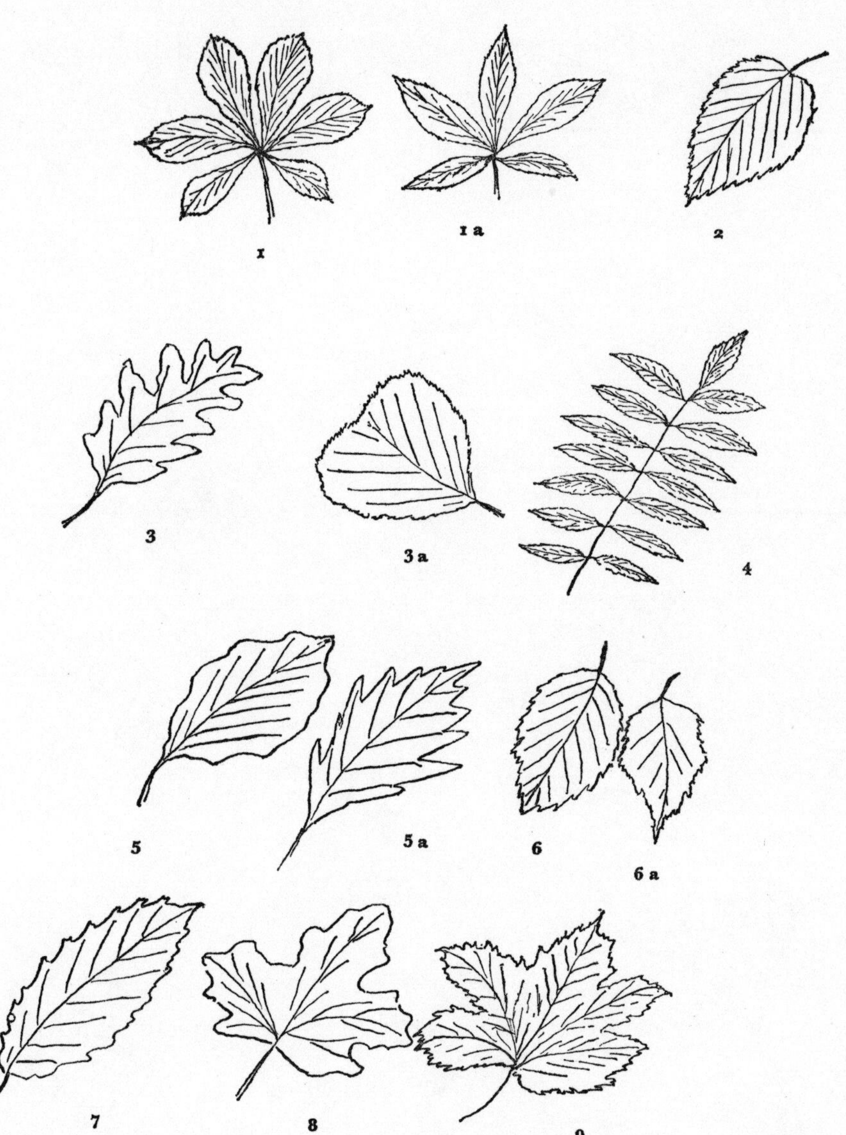

1
1 a
2
3
3 a
4
5
5 a
6
6 a
7
8
9

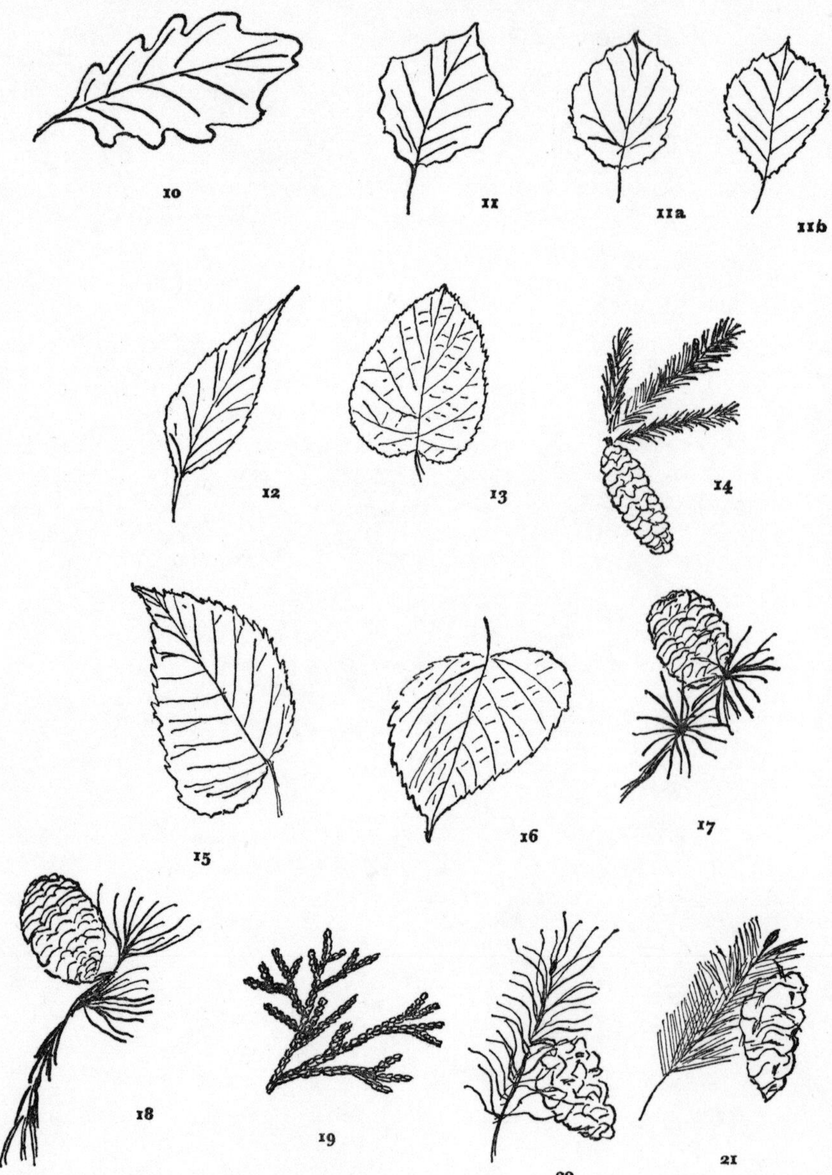
10
11
11a
11b
12
13
14
15
16
17
18
19
20
21

beach. Why not grow British miniature trees? Here, on my doorstep, was a wealth of knowledge. At that time I had not seen a British tree grown by the bonsai method. Now, when feeding mature British bonsai trees I try to get as near to the natural loam that woodland trees grow from, with slight variation. Leafmould, clay, sand and peat have the addition of manure or well-rotted garden compost. The undergrowth of woodland trees rots down each year and provides a natural growing medium, with the addition of its own leafmould.

My collection of over a hundred trees includes a few evergreens, such as cupressus, taxus and ilex, plus nearly a hundred Scotch pine seedlings, brought from Scotland in 1969. The deciduous collection includes rowan, the good old hardy chestnut, beech, oak, elm and hawthorn. Curious to see how they would grow here, in the cool greenhouse, I also have citrus fruit and date-palms – all are thriving.

Different species of certain trees have leaves of different shapes. For example, the white blossom chestnut has seven leaflets in the palmate leaf, whereas the red blossom variety has only five, slightly more pointed. The sweet chestnut is no relation to the horse chestnut and has a long leaf with serrated edges. Fig. 1 will help to distinguish many of the trees.

Once you have started, the fascination of growing minia-

Fig. 1b: 10 Oak (*Quercus*); 11 Poplar (*Populus*); 11a Aspen (*Populus tremula*); 11b Lombardy poplar (*Populas nigra var. pyramidalis*); 12 Spindle tree (*Euonymus europoeus*); 13 Wayfaring (*Viburnum lantana*); 14 Norway spruce with cone (*Picea*); 15 Elm (*Ulmus*); 16 Lime or Linden (*Tilia*); 17 Cedar of Lebanon with cone (*Cedrus libani*); 18 Indian Deodar with cone, new shoots at tip (*Cedrus deodara*); 19 Cypress (*Cupressus*); 20 Scots pine with cone (*Pinus sylvestris*); 21 Douglas fir with cone (*Pseudotsuga mensiesii*)

22
23
24
26
25
27
28
29
30
31
33
31 a
31 b
32

ture trees is beyond all imagination. To watch the planted seed break cover and then, as it is trained, to see the tiny plant slowly forming into a miniature replica of its parent plant, is like witnessing a miracle. Naturally, the training of the tree will bear a close similarity to the Japanese method; after all, the Japanese have been dwarfing trees for hundreds of years and we still have a lot to learn.

Referring to the John Innes composts in this book, each number is made up with a basic formula with nutrients added. Numbers 1, 2 and 3 formula is:

7 parts loose bulk medium loam.

2 parts coarse sand – river sand is ideal.

3 parts granulated or moss peat.

The loam should be sterilised – that is steamed for 20 minutes at a temperature of 200°F. (93°C.)

John Innes number 1, has 2 parts weight of sulphate of potash, 3 quarters ground chalk or limestone, 2 parts weight of hoof and horn and 2 parts weight of superphosphate of lime.

To J.I. number 2, add twice the amount of combined fertiliser and chalk to each bushel of loam, sand and peat. J.I. number 3, is made by adding three times the amount of nutrients.

For seed or seedling compost mix together:

1 part of bulk sand.

1 part of bulk peat.

Fig. 1c: 22 Hazel (*Corylus*); 23 Wild rose (*Rosa canina*); 24 Guelder rose (*Viburnum opulus*); 25 Holly (*Ilex*); 26 Larch with cine – new growth at tip (*Larix*); 27 Hawthorn (*Crataegus*); 28 Elder (*Sambucus nigra*); 29 Buckthorn (*Rhamnus cathartica*); 30 Crab apple (*Malus*) 31 Bay-leaved willow (*Salix pentandra*); 31a Goat willow or sallow (*Salix caprea*); 31b Weeping willow (*Salix babylonica*); 32 Walnut (*Juglans*); 33 Yew (*Taxus*)

2 parts of bulk loam – sterilised or partly sterilised. Add to each bushel $1\frac{1}{2}$ oz. superphosphate of lime. $\frac{3}{4}$ oz ground limestone or chalk. Rub through a $\frac{1}{2}$ inch mesh for a fine tilth for seed sowing.

In a number of countries these mixtures are ready made under different Trade names. Horticultural Societies, Horticultural University Departments and Educational Departments, will provide information as to trade names which vary in each country and State. In America for instance the State University of California, Horticultural Division, has the U.C. system of which some cover the J.I. formulas.

CHAPTER ONE

A SHORT HISTORY OF BONSAI TREES

China is reputed to have been the first country to develop the art of growing miniature trees. During the Sung dynasty, established in 960 A.D., the art of gardens and painting reached a high level. To the Chinese, designing gardens was a work of art. The laying of rocks in conjunction with shrubs was seen through the eye of an artist and, like an artist's view, the garden acquired an overall pattern.

Initially, miniature trees were included in tray gardens. The trays were of a curious soft stone; the tiny trees planted in them were similar in all aspects to their larger parent plant. Miniature temples, bridges, boats and figures were also included in these wondrous miniature gardens.

During the prosperous T'ang dynasty (618–907) miniature trees became known as 'the table plant' or 'dish garden', called *P'en tsai* or literally 'a green plant grown in a pot'. *P'en tsai* became *bonsai* in the Japanese pronunciation.

As the prosperity of the T'angs spread, many traders were attracted to China, including the Japanese. Chinese culture and in particular the arts; extended to other countries. Buddhism, which infiltrated from India, enhanced the art of gardening; Buddhist priests would talk for hours on the arts, including the growing of plants. By the tenth century, with the added knowledge taught by the priests, the Chinese had perfected the growing of *P'en tsai.* Although one does occasionally see a few potted trees in old Indian prints, this art never became as widespread in India as it was to become first in China, then later in Japan.

Many beautiful collections of miniature trees could still be seen in China right up to the Cultural Revolution. One wonders how many still exist. Time will tell, but it is to be hoped that some at least have been saved from vandalism and neglect. Many were hundreds of years old and today would be worth a small fortune.

It was not until the thirteenth century that the Japanese started to take the art of growing bonsai trees seriously, although bonsai was mentioned in the Kamakura period (1192–1333), as can be seen in picture scrolls illustrated with trees planted in bowls. Picture scrolls produced in the Heian period (794–1191) also show illustrations of small trees in pots. It seems likely that the Japanese had discovered the art of bonsai before the Chinese.

The Japanese, like the Chinese, regarded tray gardens and pot-gardening as one of the foremost arts of their country. Their bonsai trees were first used in their garden designs. They also knew how to lay a beautiful garden with a few rocks and appropriate plants. The miniature tree fitted perfectly into these designs.

Unlike the Chinese, the Japanese never lost interest in bonsai trees, and from a talented hobby this art has now become an export trade with markets in many countries in the world. It was not until the late eighteenth century and the beginning of the nineteenth century that bonsai trees were first seen in this country; even then, they were regarded as something of a 'gimmick', to use a modern expression. As our trade prospered, more and more boats were put to sea and, among other souvenirs, sailors would bring back these small trees for their families. It is surprising how many of the trees survived, as few knew how to look after them. Many stood for years on tables in draughty hallways, dusty, uncared for and given only an occasional drink.

During the early twentieth century, America became interested in growing bonsai trees. With Japan on the doorstep, the art spread rapidly to America and many Societies were formed. Japanese growers went to America to give talks. Books were written by the Japanese. Slowly, Britain became interested and eventually Bonsai Kai, The Japanese Society of London, was formed. It is most likely that a number of Fellows of the Royal Horticultural Society and visitors to the flower shows have seen the displays produced by the Society, for they are worth a visit at any time. There are several centres in the country which sell bonsai trees imported from Japan. In recent years, a number of growers have been concentrating on British trees. This shows the immense interest that has been aroused, however slowly, by the art of growing miniature trees, since those far-off days of the Sung dynasty when tiny trees were used in miniature tray gardens.

CHAPTER TWO

PREPARATION

Prepare the layette for the trees well in advance, for having the right-sized pot and implements at hand will save a lot of headaches. When growing from a seed or nut, you will find the half-size seed-tray adequate. It will take up to half a dozen nuts comfortably without overcrowding, making it much easier to dig out the seedling when it is ready for re-potting.

The tools required will not necessarily involve a lot of expense, except for a pair of sharp, pointed scissors and a small sharp knife. My scissors came from a Veterinary Supplier and cost very little (the most costly item in my kit). Apart from the scissors and knife, the tools to be found in the average household can be utilized. For example, the handle of an old artist's paint-brush is suitable as a comb to tease the roots; a chopstick will serve the same purpose (if you happen to have one around!). Wooden ice-cream spatulas are useful for easing compost when transplanting seedlings. A small trowel can be picked up at a chain store for around 5p. A packet of plastic labels on which to write the name and age of the tree will also be required; anchoring wire and several packets of pipe-cleaners will also be needed.

Drainage

An item essential for drainage is a collection of discs to cover the drainage holes. There are some galvanized rustproof metal discs on the market. Slightly bevelled, the discs fit nearly over the holes. But these metal discs are in short supply. Instead, a foot of fairly close mesh can be cut into one-and-a-half inch squares. Press the squares over a finger to bevel. Although the weight of the compost will flatten it a little, the disc will retain enough of its shape to give easier drainage.

Some growers use discs of foam rubber which are easy to cut to size. The snag with these is that they become sodden with water and are apt to freeze, but for trees grown in a greenhouse they are ideal. Broken crocks should be avoided, as the fibrous roots can tangle with the crocks, suffering damage when the plant is re-potted. Crocks also take up a lot of room, as well as allowing worms and insects to penetrate.

Training Wire

Pipe-cleaners are a help in the early stages of wire-training, as the soft outer cover prevents damage to the sappy branches and trunk. As they will be in use for only a short time, the rusting will do no harm. Plastic-covered wire can also be useful, although it is rather thick for delicate branches.

Containers for Growing

Containers for growing until the final potting vary in size. Initially, seeds can be planted in seed-trays or boxes. Small black polythene fold away pots are cheap and ideal for pips and nuts. Plastic drinking cups are useful, as are cream and yoghurt containers (a hot skewer will make an adequate drainage-hole in the bottom). The next sizes are as follows:

First size for seedlings $2\frac{1}{2}$ to 3 in.
Second size for potting on 3 to 4 in.
Third size for potting on 4 to 5 in.

The difference in each sizing is for plants which show quicker root-growth than others.

Composts

On the whole, the first three John Innes (JI) composts are ideal for starting and growing on the plant until the final potting.

First planting of seeds, pips and nuts–JI-seedling and JI-1

First potting of seeds, pips and nut seedling First planting of cuttings and seedlings	JI-1
Second potting of seeds, pips and nut seedlings Second potting of cuttings and seedlings	JI-1
Third potting of seeds, pips and nut seedlings Third potting of cutting and seedlings	JI-2

The third potting compost depends on the type of tree; some trees will require a stronger compost than others. Final compost will be mentioned later.

Small bags of all these composts can be purchased from garden shops and chain stores. A small bag is ample for half-size seed-trays, but for later potting (and also if you are growing more than one tree) the economy sizes will prove cheaper in the long run.

Keep all the tools and other items together, with compost and pots nearby. After use, pots should be washed in hot water to which Jeyes Fluid has been added. Hygiene is most important to prevent disease and keep the trees healthy in their small growing area.

CHAPTER THREE

GROWING A MINIATURE HORSE CHESTNUT

Horse chestnuts (*Aesculus*) are hardy little trees and can be grown easily, overwintering outside with little trouble. Although the leaves are rather large and therefore take somewhat longer to become small enough to balance the tree, this is an ideal plant with which to make a start.

In late autumn the chestnuts in their prickly pods begin to fall. The pods usually split open as they hit the ground, but the nut is left undamaged. Select several undamaged plump nuts and plant in a seed-pan. A small bag of JI-1 will be more than enough to fill a half pan. Plant the nut so that it is well covered with compost and moisten by placing the tray in water up to the rim; leave until the water has seeped through to cover the top of the compost, then take out the pan and let it drain. JI-1 is better for this type of nut, as JI-seedling seems to retard its growth a little.

On the whole, chestnuts propagate fairly quickly. In case of failure and to allow for mistakes in training, it is as well to grow several at the same time; out of these you will probably grow one good specimen.

Keep the seed pan in a cool greenhouse covered with glass or polythene, or under glass outside. The initial watering should suffice until the seedling appears; but, if the pan dries out, spray in the morning with a fine nozzle, making sure that the water soaks into the compost without making it soggy.

As soon as the first pair of true leaves appears (after the cotyledon leaves or seed-leaves), the seedling will require potting. Once again, JI-1 is used as a compost, for it is quite rich enough at this stage. Fill a three-inch pot about two-thirds full so that it is ready to take the seedling. Dig all round with the spatula, about an inch away from the seedling. Press the spatula down until you can feel the bottom of the pan, then gently push the spatula under the plant, scraping the bottom until the plant is eased away, leaving a ball of compost round the root. The nut will still be attached to the seedling; never force it away, but go on potting it until it shrivels and falls away of its own accord. You should now be able to take the small trowel, slip it underneath the seedling and transfer the seedling to the pot. Fill in the spaces round the sides with more compost, lightly pressing it down with the flat end of a pencil. Never press compost down too hard, as the plant will not be able to breathe freely. On the other hand, if the compost is too loose, the seedling will topple over. Stand the pot in a bowl of water, up to but not over the rim, until bubbles appear on the top of the compost; then take it out and let it drain.

By now the severe frosts should be over, so that the plant can stand outside under top cover, which will prevent the rain from washing out the compost. If the weather is still frosty, place the seedling under glass or in a cool greenhouse. Take it out as soon as the frosts are over, otherwise it will grow too leggy.

Chestnuts are unpredictable in their rate of growth from this stage onwards: some shoots will grow so rapidly that it will take you all your time to keep up with them. Others planted at the same time may be slower. Sometimes the slower ones are easier to handle. It sometimes happens that the trunk or stem grows as straight as a ramrod on one shoot, but on another will twist and kink. This latter tendency can be quite useful in trunk-training, a subject which will be considered shortly.

During the first leafing period, keep to three pairs of leaves. As extra pairs open, cut off the oldest pair, leaving a tiny piece of stem. This piece of stem will eventually shrivel and drop off, but by letting it die naturally you will be encouraging new leaf-growth on the stem. Continue cutting the leaves in the same way until July, when you should cease cutting until next year.

Spray the leaves with a fine spray all through the summer, either in the early morning or in the late evening (twice a day in really warm weather). Keep the plant out of very hot sun, which will scorch the leaves. As the plant needs sun to ripen the wood, filtered sun is the best, or early-morning and late-afternoon sun. Although the plant will be sprayed at least once a day, make sure that the compost is not allowed to dry out (this can easily happen in small pots during dry weather). Water as often as necessary without causing a soggy loam. To test for watering if you are not certain that the compost is dry inside, take a dry plastic label and push the end down into the compost away from the roots. In the same way as one tests the centre of a cake with a skewer to see if it is done, the label will come up clean if the compost is dry; if the compost is moist, the label will be damp with particles of compost attached.

In early October put the tree in a place where it will be sheltered from cold winds and severe frost, preferably against a wall with top cover. Clear away the leaves as they fall, to prevent slugs and other insects from hiding underneath as the leaves rot. During the winter allow the compost to dry out almost completely, then give a plunge up to the rim (never let the compost get completely dry, otherwise the tree will die). How often the tree will require watering depends on humidity, the size of pot and weather conditions. A damp winter will keep the loam moist much longer than dry or windy weather. It is most important that there is not a soggy wet mass around the roots, particularly in frosty weather. If you suspect that the soil has frozen during prolonged frosty weather, place the pot in a bath and spray with cold water until the compost has unfrozen. Leave to drain and make sure that the branches are dry; where there are evergreen leaves, ensure that these are quite dry before putting outside again.

March is a busy month for training, feeding and replacing compost when required. Taking the age of the tree from its first potting, it will now be one year old. Once again, re-pot into JI-1, which is still rich enough at this stage. Before filling with compost, place a disc over the drainage hole and then partially fill with compost (about three-quarters full). Take the chestnut carefully out of the pot by placing the hand over the top, with the first and second fingers open to place round the stem. Turn the pot over and tap the bottom

---

Fig. 2. *Miniature Horse Chestnuts*: 1 Prickly pod split after hitting the ground, showing nut inside; 2 Seedlings ready for potting, showing cotyledon leaves at the top, true pair of leaves below; 3 Second year trees in bud ready for re-potting. Note the straight and twisted stems; 4 Cut two thirds off the tap root. Trim straggling fibrous roots to dotted line to start ball of roots; 5 Cut off leaves that opened first, leaving a piece of stem; 6 Expose several roots on top with their tips under the compost. Cut out centre bud at top; 7 Continue cutting leaves to help branching. Wire train trunk. Note branching started on four-year-old tree. Leaves are nearly half the size

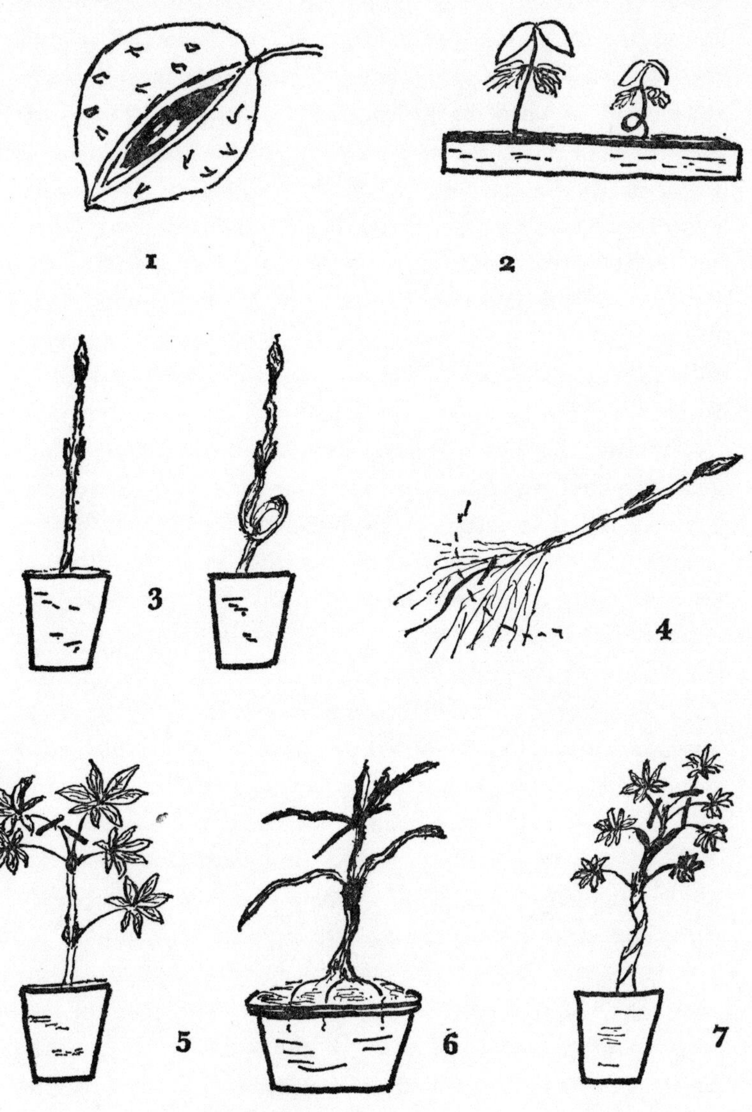

I
2
3
4
5
6
7

until the plant slides out complete with compost. With the paint-brush handle gently tease away the compost from the roots. Be very careful not to damage the top shoots. One of the best ways of carrying out this operation is to place a thick block of wood on the edge of the bench or table, turning the plant on its side with the top overhanging and holding it at the lowest part of the stem above the roots. This will prevent the top shoots from being damaged.

When the roots are clear of soil, cut two-thirds of the thicker tap root and trim any long straggling thinner roots. Compare the stem of your tiny plant and the trunk of a fully grown tree: you will notice that the grown tree has a trunk that tapers, while your plant will look very straight. To achieve this tapering effect, spread the roots out when repotting and leave a few exposed at the top. Cover the roots in the usual way, gently pressing the compost with a pencil, and then expose the lengths of four or five, keeping the tips under compost to feed the tree. As time goes on, the exposed roots will thicken to give the tree a good base. Make sure that the roots are not crossed.

Your chestnut will still have large leaves at this stage, so continue cutting as before until July. Spray through the summer and keep compost moist. Overwinter as before.

The following March, when the tree is two years old, it will again need re-potting in JI-1 (the method is the same). Trim straggling roots and cut out the rest of the tap root. Keep the same roots exposed, making sure that the feeding tips are under the compost. As the leaves unfold, you may now notice that they are appreciably smaller; continue cutting up to July. Should some of the leaves be larger than others, cut away about a third of each of these until they, in turn, are cut right out.

In March of the third year re-pot into JI-2. If the trunk

appears stiff and straight, join together several pipe-cleaners at the tips by cleaning a little of the fluff away and twisting the wire together. Thread the cleaners through the bottom hole and the disc up above the line of compost. More pipe-cleaners can be added if required. Attach the bottom of the cleaner by twisting it round a label so that it lies flat across the hole. About a month after the tree has been potted, twist the cleaner gently and evenly round the trunk, gradually bending the trunk into shape. The wire should touch without being tight. Always wire in the direction you wish the tree to bend : to the right if a bend to the right side is required and vice versa. Take the wire off in September and re-wire again the following year, using copper wire. If you feel that the trunk needs wiring in the second year, apply the same method with the pipe-cleaners two years running. After wiring, apply a pinch of dried blood and in October a pinch of bonemeal. A pinch between the fingers is ample (over-feeding will cause a lot of lush growth which is difficult to deal with and can kill a tree).

When the tree is four years old, it will begin to look much more interesting in shape and can be potted into final containers.

CHAPTER FOUR

PRUNING

Root Pruning

Large parent-trees depend for their size on the root-growth under ground: a balance is established between the roots and the trunk and branches. This also applies to bonsai trees and the balance must be maintained to keep a healthy green head. The roots suck up moisture to the upper growth and so a small root formation gives less top growth. Without this balance, the tree will sap its strength, begin to look weakly and probably die.

Root pruning takes place at the time of re-potting. Even though the growth may be on the small side, cutting back straggling roots and just tipping the rest will encourage thicker growth.

Plants grown from seed should have the tap-root cut by two thirds at one year old; the rest is cut away at two years. At the same time, trim fibrous roots. Some species have a much quicker root-growth and may be almost pot-bound by the time they are re-potted. In the third and fourth years the roots will thicken. Cut back to a thick ball, except for the two or three roots required for the top of the container and roots that are to be trained over a rock. Trim the latter back to a suitable length so that they straddle the rock.

On the whole deciduous trees will require re-potting every two or three years from the age of four years. If there are any signs of roots coming up through the loam or pushing

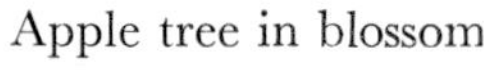

Apple tree in blossom

Chinese juniper, eleven years old, with 'daughter'

A young hazel tree

Twenty-five-year-old maple

their way through the bottom between these times, re-pot and trim the roots.

Leaf Pruning

Leaf pruning for the larger-leaved trees has been described in Chapter 3. Later, as the growth becomes more prolific, it may be necessary to cut out overcrowded or intercrossing leaves. If the growth is too lush, cut the feed to half. Where leaves are not required to replace themselves, cut right down to the branch or branchlet. If leaves are to be replaced, leave a small piece of stem when you cut.

On large-leaved trees, such as the chestnut, the leaf itself is cut to correspond with the smaller annual growth. With trees whose parents have smaller leaves, such as the beech, it is not necessary to leaf-cut, but it is important to cut out leaves, making sure that you allow a piece of stem to remain. The object of cutting out leaves is to encourage growth and to give a good healthy head with leaves corresponding to the size of the tree.

Where there is an abundance of leaves, cut out alternate leaves in the thickest part, down to the wood. If leaves require replacing or a branch is thinly leaved, cut leaves so that a piece of stem remains.

The maple is one of the few trees that can have two or three leaf-falls, which means that the size of the leaves is reduced much faster. Before attempting an artificial 'fall', make sure that the tree is healthy and growing well.

Once the leaves are fully out, cut them all off, leaving a piece of stem. Repeat this procedure in the middle of the summer when the tree is in leaf again. The third fall, in the autumn, will be the natural fall. Apply these artificial 'falls' when the tree is four to five years old. The following year there will be a noticeable difference in the size of the leaves.

If they still need reducing, give one artificial fall during the year.

The elm is another tree that can have one artificial fall in its first flourish of leaf (repeat the following year if necessary).

Bud Pruning

Take a good look at the tree in the bud stage in late winter or early spring. Adequate feeding and potting should not only produce vigorous roots but enliven branches, which will bring forth new buds. To prevent the tree from being overburdened, some of these buds may need rubbing out. Except in the case of beech and maple, you should nip out unwanted buds between April and September. As you become more experienced you will be able to rub out the buds before leaf-break, leaving an adequate number to produce a good head. Beech and maple should be treated in the same way in March. Also, nip all bud-growth that has gone beyond the line of the branches.

Pinching Out

Once again, you should wait for a few weeks after repotting before pinching out. Allow the main centre stem or trunk to grow to the height required, taking into consideration the root-growth. This also applies to the branches, which must balance the centre trunk; when it is tall enough, pinch out the centre of the trunk and branches.

On fruit trees rub out unwanted buds before they start to shoot, leaving half-a-dozen blossoming buds on a small branch. Clusters of flowers and berries should be pinched out, so that three or four are left in each cluster, with no more than two clusters to the branch.

About a month after leaf-break a number of new sprouts

from the branches will be noticeable. Those that are to be kept should have the centre pinched out when three inches long. This will ensure that the next growth of leaves will be smaller and it also assists the growth of the branchlet. The last pinching, in late August, will be checked by the cooler weather. Continue pinching during the growing season. Once the season is over, you will be able to check the balance of the tree.

Where long and short shoots appear on the same branch,

Fig. 3. *Viburnum*. No more than two clusters of berries on each branch. Split trunk with main branches

pinch the shorter one first; then, a couple of weeks later, pinch the centre of the longer one. The shorter shoot will have almost caught up by this time.

Branch Pruning

After re-potting and root pruning, wait at least four weeks before attempting to prune branches. The unwanted branches are those that are overcrowding one another or are crossed over another branch; unhealthy branches and those which have grown out of shape should also be pruned. Always use a sharp implement to make a clean cut. With branches on the thick side that are likely to leave a scar, leave a tiny piece of branch about one-tenth of an inch long, then whittle small pieces away during the summer, until the trunk is smooth.

Overcrowding branchlets growing from the main branch and branchlets that cross should be cut down to the stem on deciduous trees, except in the case of fruit and flowering trees. Fruit and flowering trees, such as the prunus, the apple and berried trees, should be pruned in the dormant season (late autumn or early winter). Branches should be kept short so that they bear an even quantity of blossom and fruit. Other unwanted branches or branchlets should be cut clean at the base. To shorten branches, select a bud on the outside of the branch and cut on the slant inwards, in the same way that roses are pruned. After cutting woody branches, dab the scar with one of the proprietary brands of sealing paint to prevent infection and to stop unwanted insects burrowing into the centre.

Spray the tree with a fine spray after treatment, whether it has been leaved, pruned, pinched out or branch-pruned. Whenever possible, use soft water, even if you have to catch the rain in a bucket. Chemicals in town supplies tend to leave a hard whitish line; the continuous use of town water on the small amount of loam in the container builds up the chemical output, which could be detrimental to the tree.

Conifers

New growth on the majority of conifers is noticeable by the lighter green. Needle trees, such as the pine, have thickish buds at the tip. Pinch out about two-thirds at the first pinching and the rest a couple of weeks later. Cut overlong branches back to a node. Should the needless appear too long for the size of the branch, trim back about one-third.

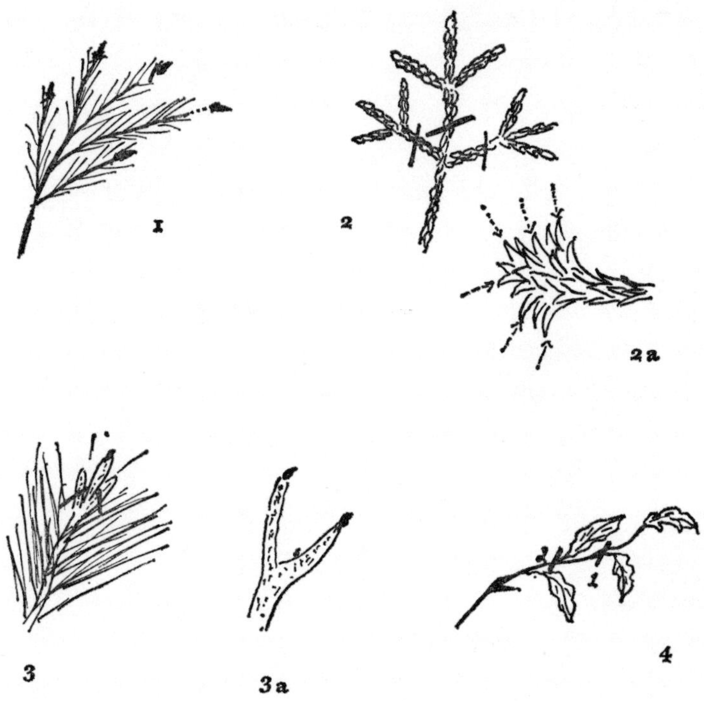

Fig. 4. *Pinching out, cutting and leaf pruning*: 1 Pinch out buds on spruce as they appear; 2 Cut the new growth of cypress, leaving small piece of growth; 2a Pinch out new leaves as they appear after cutting; 3 Nip two thirds of pine buds at first pinching, complete two weeks later; 3a Shows new branchlet growth after nipping; 4 Cut leaves on deciduous trees to first node; then, two weeks later to second node

Spruce has a bud at the tip and the bud should be pinched out as it appears. Cut back new growth one-third at a time.

Junipers can be trimmed in the same way by nipping off the buds as they appear.

Cupressus will show its new growth with a lighter fresh green and in the shape of a Y. When pinching out, leave a tiny piece of the lighter green, otherwise growth may be retarded.

CHAPTER FIVE

USEFUL HINTS

Keeping a Diary

Nothing is more frustrating than not being able to remember the exact date when the tree was pruned, pinched out or fed and re-potted, its age and other treatment given, particularly when growing several different types or species. Keeping a diary will give you a record of all these details and will also be a great help where mistakes in treatment may have been made. As you become more versatile in growing bonsai trees, you will notice how individual they can become. The following method of keeping track of all treatment and training has proved infallible in my own experience.

Write the number on the label and also mark it indelibly on the container so that it will not be washed off. This will ensure that, if the label is lost, the number is available for reference to the diary. Say, for instance, your chestnut is No. 1: write 'No. 1' on the label and on the container or pot at each re-potting. Then head your page in the diary as follows:*

TREE	DATE	POT	COMPOST	FEED	AGE
No. 1	10/66	Sown	JI-1		
Chestnut	3/67	P.	JI-1		5 months

*Abbreviations: P.: Potted. C.: Final container. D.B.: Dried blood. F.C.: Final compost. B.M.: Bone-meal. L.M.: Liquid manure. Fill: Filling in with compost without re-potting.

TREE	DATE	POT	COMPOST	FEED	AGE
TYPE	3/68	P.	JI-1		1 year
Nut	3/69	P.	JI-1		2 years
	3/70	P.	JI-2	D.B.	3 years
	3/71	C.	F.C.		4 years
	10/71			B.M.	
	3/72		Fill	D.B.	5 years
	6/72			L.M.	
	10/72			B.M.	

On the opposite side of the page, enter dates of wire training, branch cutting and any other relevant data.

Final Compost

Some trees will grow happily in JI-2 with the addition of dried blood, bone-meal and a few drops of liquid manure. If it is possible to obtain the following ingredients, you will find that they improve the trees:

Put through a quarter-inch sieve:

1 part leafmould
1 part peat
¼ part washed sand
¼ part well-rotted manure or garden compost
1 part loam
¼ part dried clay

Mix well together, then sieve again. This time use the wire-mesh kitchen sieve. Place the coarser mixture left in the sieve at the bottom of the container and the finer mixture on the top.

An old flower-pot with the hole cemented makes an ideal container in which to measure out the parts. Fill it for one part and then the halves and quarters can be measured accordingly. For my large number of trees I use a two-gallon plastic bucket.

Containers for Final Potting

When trees are ready for their final potting the right type of container will be required. In this country reasonably priced vessels for this purpose are not easily obtainable, although with one or two trees it will be worth buying the Japanese bonsai type of container. The ordinary reddish clay flower-pot has a tendency to crack in frost, whereas the dark, hard-baked vessels made specially for bonsai trees are hard enough to withstand frosts. If you are really stuck, plastic seed-trays slightly raised on flat stones or a dab of cement will prove adequate initially. A container made of

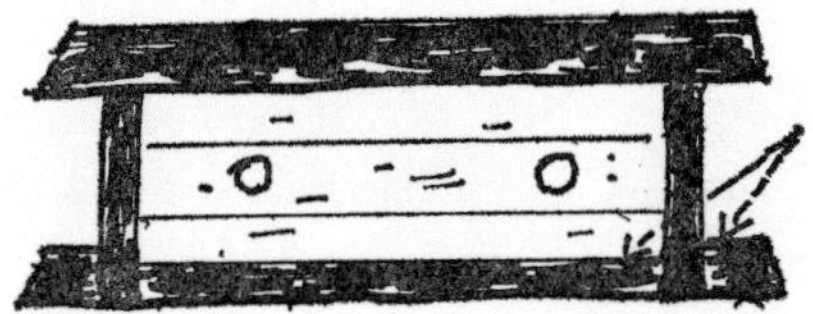

Fig. 5. *Home-made wooden container.* The centre is fixed above the bottom level as indicated by the arrows. Thus, the side frames also make the feet

wood will last for several years. Choose a wood with an interesting grain, joining it together like a seed-tray and keeping the two side-pieces longer to give an oriental appearance. The side-pieces should overlap at the bottom to raise the container from the ground. Drill two holes in the centre, one towards each end. An interesting and cheap form of container can thus be made, the size depending on the tree.

The colours of containers should enhance the tree, although this is a matter of individual choice. Bright colours and patterns will detract from the beauty of the plant; monochrome is better in most cases. Glazing should be on the outside only, not inside or underneath.

Light coloured flowers match with pale cream or greenish

containers. Light green foliage is better with deeper green or dark blue. Brightly coloured fruits show to advantage with deep clayish brown and other nondescript colours.

The size of the container should be in proportion to the size of the tree. The height of the tree is the important factor. Keep the container about two-thirds the height of the tree.

Strong trees, such as the oak, require containers with an appearance of strength, whereas the prunus needs a container of lighter appearance. When planting in final containers, keep the tree to one side. Imagine a frame with the container and tree as the theme, filling in the canvas to give an overall picture.

The shape of the container should harmonize with the shape of the tree. A single straight tree looks better in a fairly deep rectangular container. An oval shape harmonizes with a bonsai with two trunks. Groups of trees should be planted in a circular or oval container of shallow shape. Drooping or 'Cascade' trees should be set in deep square pots. Shallow trays are also better for trees grown over rocks.

CHAPTER SIX

WIRING AND TRAINING TECHNIQUES

Stand the tree at eye level and take a good look at the trunk and branches, turning it round slowly. You may find that the trunk is too straight or bends in the wrong places, either too high or too low. The branches may be out of alignment, spoiling the overall design of the tree.

Providing that re-potting has taken place at least a month beforehand, the wire training can commence. Most trees can be wired between April and June. Pines are better wired during these months, or between October and January.

Before re-potting, anchor a piece of wire under the pot with a label, so that the wire comes about half an inch above the loam. After the initial stages of wiring with pipe-cleaners, copper wire will be necessary as the trunk and branches thicken up. Lead wire is a good substitute. The thickness of copper wire required ranges from No. 12 to No. 16. It may be necessary to use No. 18 on an older tree. Use a thinner wire to start with; if you find it is not adequate, change to a thicker one at the next re-wiring. Wire must be pliable. To make copper wire easy to handle, throw it on the red embers of a fire or perch it over a gas ring or electric plate. It will regain its rigidity after wiring.

When the wire is ready for use, twist the end together with the anchoring piece sticking out of the loam. Now turn the wire evenly right up the trunk, keeping it close to the trunk, but on no account bind tightly, otherwise it will scar.

Before wiring, take the trunk in your hand and gently bend to the required shape. Should the trunk be hard or

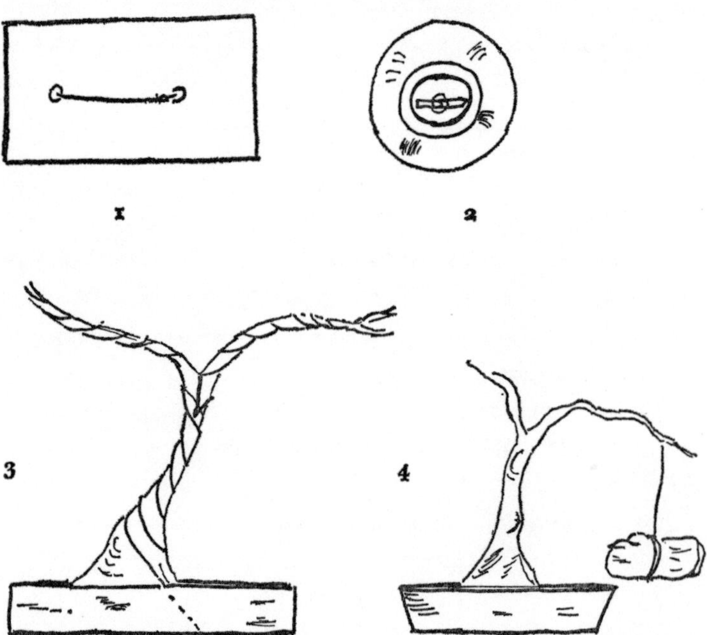

Fig. 6. *Anchoring wire*: 1 Wire anchored by passing through two holes and twisting it underneath one; 2 For containers with one hole, twist end of wire around label; 3 Wire for training branches is anchored to trunk wire by pushing underneath and turning up; 4 Weighing a branch with a stone instead of wiring

brittle, make a shallow cut where it is to bend before wiring.

To anchor the wire for branches, give it a turn at the base of the branch and tuck in the end. Bend the branches to the shape required and wire in the same way as for the trunk.

Some trees have thin or sappy stems which could easily

be damaged. To prevent marking, cover the wire or the stem with soft paper before wiring. Turn the wire in the direction in which the tree is to bend : to the right if the bend is to go towards the right and vice versa. After wiring, gently twist the branch or trunk in the direction that it is wired. Spray the top each day and keep out of sunlight for a few days.

If you prefer, you can copy the shapes for your trees from

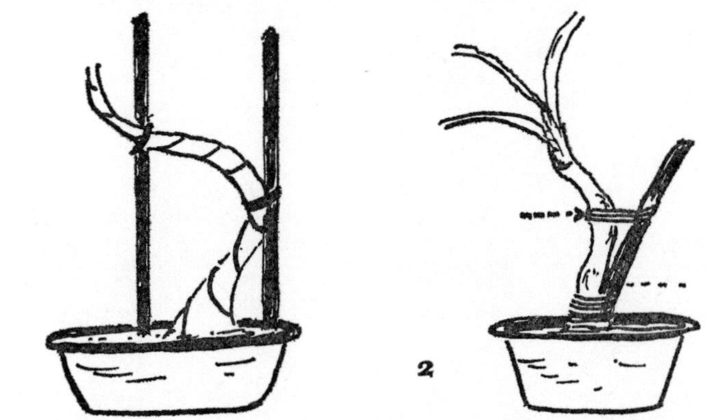

Fig. 7. *Further ways of bending a trunk* : 1 Trunk attached to supports where bend is required; 2 Metal stake bound to tree at bottom. A hard rubber pad is pushed between stake and trunk, then tied above. A second pad is used to prevent wire cutting the bark. Both pads are indicated by arrows

the woodland species. On the other hand, one cannot go far wrong in selecting shapes in the Japanese styles. The most simple method is the 'Lines of Beauty' used in *Ikebana,* the Japanese art of flower arranging. This design has three main branches: the centre stem (or trunk in the case of a tree) is known as 'Heaven', with 'Man' to the left and 'Earth' to the right. This is a simple formation and easy to control.

Hankan style gives a tree the appearance of having been bent by the wind. After wiring the trunk by the same method as before, bend it first to one side and then to the other. Never bend back to front. This style requires early training, which should begin in the third or fourth year while the

Fig. 8. *Beech with split trunk.* This upright style has an interestingly shaped trunk which has been achieved by allowing a branch to grow from the top side of the trunk. Beech is an ideal tree to split as it quickly throws thick branches from the base

Fig. 9. *Hankan.* Few branches are allowed to grow, otherwise the tree will look over-fussy. This styles requires a long trunk bent from side to side – not back to front

trunk is still pliable. Only two or three branches should be kept, otherwise it will look fussy.

There are two ways of growing a forest of trees. In the *Ikadi-Buki* style the trunk of the tree is trained horizontally, with the branches standing up to give the appearance of many trees. Cut off the bottom branches of a dormant tree and the leading shoot. Partly bury the main trunk and roots, first cutting off the branches underneath and making sure that the upper branches have dormant buds. Train the upper branches and, if necessary, cut some out if they are overcrowded.

Another way to make a forest of trees, *Yoseue*, is to grow a number of trees of different species in pots and with varying

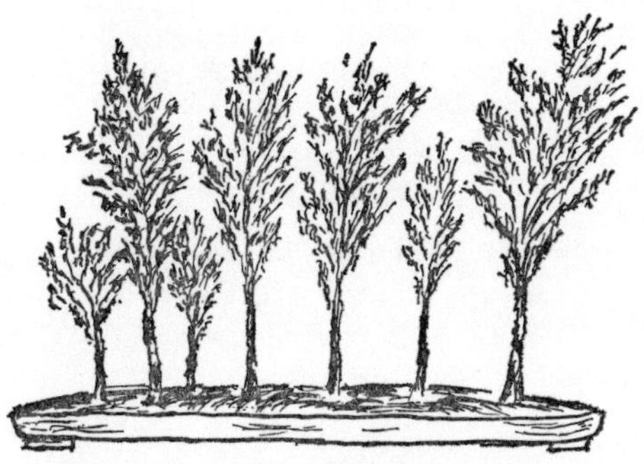

Fig. 10. *Yoseue (Forest of Trees) for collective planting.* Raised bed containing a forest of beech trees. Collective planting is ideal for trees with narrow trunks, Scots pine, birch and beech among others

heights and thicknesses. If they are grown in the wide-topped clay pots used for cuttings, they can be left until they are ready to take their place in the final container. Train them to the upright style, bending the trunks a little at various angles so that they do not appear too uniform. For this style an oval tray is best. Plant the tallest tree about one-third from one end of the tray and the next tallest at the opposite end. Now plant five or six more at intervals, without making them look uniform. Trim the roots before planting into the tray and generally tidy up the trees. The following year, train the trees as necessary with copper wire. Cut out any branches that intertwine and also unwanted branchlets. Nip the new growth in the spring.

Fig. 11. *Cascade crab apple.* An easy style for fruit trees, particularly crab apple. Note the balance of the branches. The rather straight trunk is ideal for well-marked wood

Fig. 12. *Weeping willow.* As if blown over by a gale, the willow weeps from three main branches. An ideal style for any weeping or natural cascading growth – weeping elm for example. The tip of the branches should be kept upright to allow weeping branchlets to fall around the branch

The *Kengai* or 'Cascade' style is not as difficult as it looks. The easiest way to achieve this falling effect is to fit through the pot a thick piece of stout wire just over twice as long as

Beech tree

Another beautiful old maple

Thirty-year-old trident maples growing over rocks. Between them – a tiny *Mame* maple

An impressive group of Sequoias, with one tiny cotoneaster in the middle. The trees are from twelve to fifteen years in age

the pot. Place the pot on the edge of a bench or table and then bend the wire over the rim until the end is below the bottom of the pot. Plant a young tree with a pliable trunk in the container. At intervals along the trunk tie raffia over small rubber pads, then tie the raffia to the wire, bending the tree little by little. Tighten the raffia a little each month until the desired effect is achieved. You will find that the branches will

Fig. 13. *Holly.* The basic shape has been achieved. Branches require pinching back and the two top ones further shaping

need training to a different angle; wire the branches a month after potting. To anchor the tree in the pot, bind strong wire round the outside of the pot and across the roots; place foam or rubber mats over the roots to prevent scarring. Once the roots have taken hold, the wire can be removed.

Keep an alert eye on wired trees in case tightening or bulging occurs. As soon as there is any sign of this, cut away the wire and re-wire the following year. On young trees the interval between cutting away the wire and re-wiring will allow the sap to flow freely and fill out the stem, thus eradicating any scarring. On older trees it can take years for scars to disappear and sometimes they never vanish completely.

Another method of curving a tough trunk is using a 'jack'. First place a piece of rubber at the lower end of the trunk, then bind a stout piece of metal to the trunk. The metal should be as tall as the trunk and strong enough not to bend. Push a piece of rubber down between the metal and the trunk (the rubber will pull the metal away from the trunk at the top); then bind the top of the metal tightly, placing a small pad on the outside of the trunk. This method will give a bend to the trunk between the lower binding and the opening at the top.

For branches that are growing too straight, weights can be used. This is one of the oldest methods of 'hanging' branches and is ideal for sensitive or sappy trees and for very old trees. Simply attach string or raffia to the part of the tree which you wish to correct and add a weight to the other end. To 'hang' the branch, fix the string at the tip. This is an ideal method for those who are not too confident of their ability to wire tender branches.

In Chapter 3 it was pointed out that the trunk of a chestnut will often twist as it grows. As the twist is usually fairly low down, you should curve the straight part of the trunk with wire, otherwise it will look like a candle on a Christmas tree. Often, sowing the nut on its side will result in a twist. At other times it will twist of its own accord, even when sown in the usual manner. Just why some stems twist in this way is impossible to say, particularly as chestnuts normally grow very straight with thick trunks.

CHAPTER SEVEN

GROWING AN OAK TREE

What a wealth of history the oak trees have! The oak was used to build the man-o'-war and to prop up buildings that have lasted through the centuries; craftsmen have used it to make furniture that has stood the test of time. Oak is a wood that hardens with age, hence its long life. It is sad to see these great and beautiful trees, which take a generation and more to reach their full glory, come crashing down in the name of progress. There will come a time when the oak will be merely a tourist attraction in parks and show gardens, when youngsters will look upon this tree as part of history.

At least we can show our grandchildren what an oak is, if we grow one in miniature. The oak is a slow grower and it will take some time to show its full beauty. But, once mature, it will prove a priceless heritage.

During the autumn, as the acorns fall, select half a dozen plump nuts and place them in a seed-pan, as for the chestnut, potting on when the first pair of true leaves appears. Oak seedlings are better without too much disturbance. In the first year, instead of re-potting, take about an inch of compost off the top and replace with fresh JI-1.

At two years old, re-pot in JI-1, cutting back half the tap-root. In October, add a pinch of bone-meal. In March of the following year, add JI-2 to the top inch instead of re-potting.

As the oak will not be sufficiently mature to go into a

final container in its fourth year, transfer it to a shallow, wide-topped cutting pot, where it can be allowed to grow on for several more years. At the same time, cut out the rest of the tap-root and pot into JI-2. Trim the fibrous roots lightly, leaving two or three exposed with the tips just buried.

By the following year the leaves will be thickening. Keep four on each spray, cutting out the first to open and leaving

Fig. 14. *Young oak after spring pruning, ready to be rewired.* This tree is still undergoing intensive training

the piece of stem. As side-shoots appear, pinch out the centre only. Spray continually through the summer.

An oak needs wire training before the wood hardens. As oaks are such slow growers, with the trunk staying spindly for some time, wire training will start later than for most other trees. Yet it is surprising how different conditions and climate in various parts of the country affect the growth. As soon as the stem starts to thicken or any signs of hardening of the trunk appear, start wire training (in April or October).

Leave the tree in the clay pot for several more years,

putting fresh compost on the top every other year, re-potting in between and at the same time trimming the fibrous roots. In June, give a feed of liquid manure (four drops to a pint of water).

When the oak is large enough to look interesting, move it into its final container. The oak looks well in a deep vessel – dark blue is a good colour. It is not a delicate tree and there-

Fig. 15. *Chokkan (upright style)*. This style of tree looks well in its skeleton state during the winter. Its appearance is one of strength, so is associated with the oak. It is a style suitable for bonsai trees where the parent tree is large. Note the strong branches with branchlets at the end. These are pinched back and cut out when in leaf, to give an all-over style

fore should not be placed in a delicate container. Carry on training and pruning as for other mature trees.

Oaks look much more natural if trained in the *Chokkan* or upright style, with thick exposed roots to give power and breadth to the trunk. Gnarl the thicker branches by bending the wire and keeping them close-cropped. Then allow the thinner branchlets from the main branches to spread – this will give the thick head that the oak grows naturally. Fig.

15 shows how few large branches are required: the leafing branches growing from the main branches provide the head.

Although this is an upright style, the trunk is wired in the early stages to prevent a stiff shaping; at the same time, it is only slightly curved, the power being in the thickness of the trunk.

CHAPTER EIGHT

LOOKING AFTER MATURE TREES

Root pruning is the chief factor in keeping the tree in its miniature state. As it gets older and providing the roots have been adequately pruned in the earlier years, it will not require pruning so often. If there are any signs of roots growing through the compost or the bottom of the pot, cut back as far as possible with a pair of sharp pointed scissors, then root prune and re-pot in March.

Trees need annual re-potting up to the age of four years, then every other year to the age of ten, unless they are not making a great deal of root-growth, in which case they should be left for an extra year after the age of four. At ten years old, root prune and then re-pot every four years. During this four-year period the tree will still require fresh compost in small doses. The easiest method is to cut a square of the old compost out from the side of the pot, taking care not to damage the roots, particularly the thicker-roots, and then fill in with fresh compost. When the tree is watered, the nutriment from the fresh compost will soon reach the roots. At the same time sprinkle a pinch of dried blood round the roots.

In June each year give a dose of liquid manure (four drops to a pint of water, or two drops to half a pint, depending on the size of container). Pour slowly over the top of the compost to enable the liquid to soak right through. In October, stir in a pinch of bone-meal.

Continue leaf cutting where necessary. Pinch out shoots and cut out unwanted branchlets. Prune fruit and berried trees in the dormant season. Take out dead and unwanted branches. Some growers leave old dead branches on a tree to give it an aged appearance. This is not always wise, as the wood can be a breeding-place for disease and unwanted insects. Diseases can spread quickly on these small trees and it is safer to cut out old branches. Train new shoots to take their place or replace by grafting.

Continue spraying the tree in warmer weather, making sure it is not allowed to dry out. Hardy trees must be kept outside, either on shelves or on a pedestal.

Easing out Trees from Containers

Some difficulty is often experienced in easing out trees planted in final containers, and especially those planted in trays. Gently loosen the compost round the edges with a spatula, then place your hand flat on the top of the compost with fingers splayed round the trunk. With the thicker trunks, use the thumb and first finger. Turn the container on its side and smartly tap the bottom. On no account pull the tree: let it gradually loosen itself from the pot. For older trees with thicker trunks and also for a 'forest' of trees, remove as much compost as possible, taking care not to damage the roots; then turn the container on its side and tap the bottom. Another pair of hands is useful to hold the top growth, leaving yours free to handle the container.

Bud-drop

If buds start to drop, the cause is often dry conditions.

Make sure the compost is moist in late winter when the buds are forming.

Leaf-drop Before Time

When leaves drop before their time, the cause may be either too little or too much water, and sometimes overfeeding. Examine the compost for sogginess or dryness and adjust accordingly. If the top is growing lush, cut down liquid manure to half and every other year add the pinch of bonemeal.

Brown Marks on Leaves

These can either be scorch marks from too much hot sun or the result of hot sun on wet leaves. Overwatering can also affect the leaves. Cut off the brown marks and move the tree into a shady place for the rest of the summer, making sure that the compost is not soggy.

To Sum Up

Keep shelves clean and spray regularly with pyrethrum, which will deter as well as kill unwanted pests. Pyrethrum is quite harmless to warm-blooded creatures and the safest insecticide to use, particularly where there are family pets and young children.

Cut out dead or badly damaged branches on otherwise healthy trees, thus avoiding further spread of infection, should this be the cause. Dead and withered leaves should also be cut off. If possible, when there is cause to suspect infection, separate the tree from its companions until it has recovered.

Overwatering can do untold harm, particularly in the winter. A dried-out container can kill. Overfeeding will cause lush growth and a sapping of the tree's strength. Insufficient food will make for a dreary, dull tree and will eventually kill it.

A little food given at intervals is better than a lot at once. It can always be topped up if necessary. An overfed plant is the hardest to combat; on the other hand, a shrivelled plant will almost certainly die. Patience is required, but the reward is well worth the effort.

Summer and Winter Quarters

When growing a collection of trees, it is essential that they have somewhere to stand in the summer and a frost-free place in the winter. If you are lucky enough to have a wall within easy access of the house (this is important for your own well-being, as it is not much fun trudging through snow and heavy rain to inspect the trees each day), it is easy to fix shelves on the wall with brackets. The top and sides can be slatted to allow a little rain to penetrate; or, if you wish to control the water, cover the top with polythene. Build the shelves in tiers (the widest at the bottom and the narrowest at the top). In a fierce winter a polythene curtain can be fixed, like a curtain on stretch-wire rods.

Where there are only a few trees, a wooden tea trolly with props fitted at the side to take the cover will serve the same purpose. The advantage of a trolly is that it can be wheeled to any part of the garden and turned against cold winds.

During the summer months the trees can be displayed on pedestals in the garden. Make sure that they are firm enough not to be blown over by a wind or knocked down by cats. Rocks make appropriate stands: large rocks with flat tops should be used for the larger trees, while the smaller containers can be wedged in by smaller rocks. Rocks help to create a Japanese setting ideal for showing the trees to their best advantage.

Except for citrus fruit-trees and trees which are not hardy in this country, do not coddle your trees – just protect them from unduly fierce weather, such as heavy rain, which might wash out the loam and also break tender branches, and hot continuous sunshine. Trees must also be sheltered from very cold winds, particularly when they are young.

Disease and Pests

On the whole, bonsai trees are not prone to disease as long as they are kept in a healthy condition. There are exceptions and, prevention being better than cure, is as well to take a few basic precautions.

Apple-trees are susceptible to mildew, so it is wise to spray with Karathane in the spring. 'Spraydex', which is sold in a spray container, is a useful stand-by for use during the summer, should the mildew reappear (The refills are about half the price of the original container.)

Aphides can be a nuisance. Pyrethrum used in a spray once a week will usually keep them away. It is also effective on ants and woodlice. It is quite harmless to warm-blooded creatures (even bees do not seem to worry when they are accidently sprayed).

Red spider mite can be prevented by spraying with Malathon. They are not often seen on bonsai trees, but are fatal when they do attack.

Providing the hole at the bottom of the pot is adequately covered with a disc, worms should not be able to enter the container. If there is any suspicion of worms in the compost, turn the tree out and fill with fresh compost.

A heavy crop of woodlice can be cleared with BHC.

Keep the area clear of fallen leaves and other debris, the loam sweet and the trees sprayed, to protect your trees from disease and pests.

CHAPTER NINE

USE OF MOSS, ROCKS AND STONES

Bonsai trees grown in trays look much more natural with moss growing on the top of the compost. Moss also helps to keep the compost moist. Soak sphagnum moss thoroughly in soft water and then gently squeeze out the surplus. Place a thin layer of peat over the compost right up to the exposed roots, then cover the peat with the moss. The peat will help to bind the moss, preventing it from lifting or from being washed away when the tree is watered. After laying the moss, give it a good watering with a fine spray. Moss should be laid when wire is off the branches and trunk and about three or four weeks after giving fresh compost or re-potting. Continue wire training the following year.

Rocks and Stones

Placing rocks and stones of suitable sizes in strategic positions in the container does suggest a certain ruggedness of scenery. For small trees, stones should be used. The rocks for the larger trees should not be so big that they obliterate the beauty of the tree.

Choose rocks or stones with interesting grain and colour. Rocks with hollows to hold water are ideal for water-loving trees such as the willow. Rugged rocks from Scotland look well with mountain ash or rowan. Rocks with strong veining are suitable for oaks and chestnuts.

Growing Trees over Rocks

Any tree that is to be grown over a rock should be selected when quite young; the roots should be allowed to grow instead of being cut back, although they should be lightly trimmed at the tips. During the re-potting years, cut back and eventually cut away the tap-root, any dead or broken roots, and also a few in the centre. The ideal time for planting the tree over a rock is just before budding, when the tree is five to six years old.

Select a rock which is fairly rough in texture with grooves and crevices to allow the roots to grip the rock. On the whole, small-leafed trees with several branches making a thick head are better than a tree with one or two heavy branches. Evergreens are ideal for this style, and especially conifers, although a mountain ash will look perfectly natural in this position.

The rock can have either a peak top, a dipped top or a flat top, depending on the type and style of tree to be grown over it. For instance, a mountain ash can have a peak or rugged top, as it grows in the rugged rocks of Scotland and is often seen high on a peak.

Under the broadest part of the rock chip out a few small holes alternately, one above the other and all the way round. Fill in with a dab of cement; then, just before it dries, push in a panel-pin slanting downwards. Leave to harden and then soak the whole rock in soft water.

Trays should be used for this style to show the whole to the best advantage. Anchor a fairly long piece of plastic-covered wire under the holes, bringing it up through the tray. Fill the tray with compost and place the stone in position.

Bear in mind the shape of the tree to achieve an overall effect. Place the tree on the rock, straddling the roots over the side and making sure they are long enough to go under the compost. If they are too long, it is better to double them back under the compost than to cut them off. Take the double plastic-covered wire round the rock and over the roots, giving it a twist at each panel-pin. This will anchor the roots and prevent the tree from rocking.

Cover the roots at the lower part with compost, firming

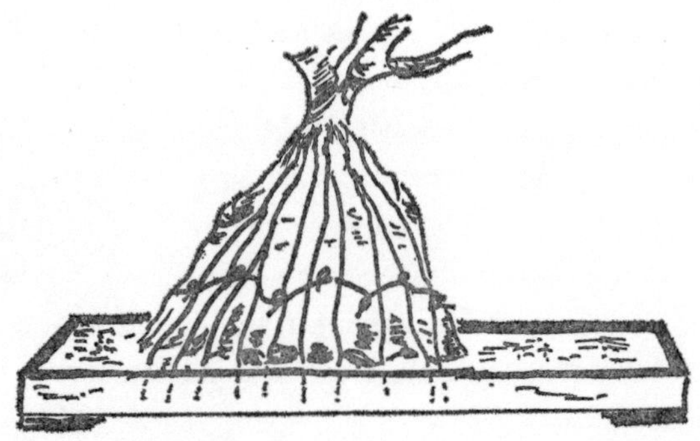

Fig. 16. *Planting over a stone is achieved by pins attached to the rock.* Roots straddle over the rock and are anchored with plastic-covered wire with a twist on each pin. Tips of the roots under compost are show by dots

it gently. Mould a portion of clay with a little water (just enough to make it stick) and cover the exposed roots on the rock. If you have any difficulty in making the clay stick, cover with sphagnum moss and bind firmly with wire without cutting into the moss, otherwise the wire will eventually cut the roots; keep the moss damp. When the clay appears to be holding, spray and gently peel the moss away.

At the next re-potting, which may be two or more years later, take off a piece of clay nearest to the trunk. If the roots have thickened, remove clay from under the trunk and the following year remove the rest. In the meantime, if the clay has crumbled, it will do no harm if it drops off, providing the roots have thickened. On the other hand, if the roots are still thin and hairy, add more clay as before.

When re-potting trees over rocks, take care to hold the tree and the rock together. Two pairs of hands are better than one during this operation.

CHAPTER TEN

DIFFERENT METHODS OF GROWING

For digging up mature trees a sharp-bladed tool or keen-edged spade will be necessary. You will also need a trowel with a long narrow blade or a three-pronged fork, for clearing under roots; a long bladed knife and secateurs; sacking for wrapping round the roots; polythene bags, string and raffia; plenty of moss and a water container – and a hefty pair of muscles!

Seedlings

Parent trees cast their seeds or nuts, which can often be found growing under the base of the tree. Oak, elm, chestnut, ash and conifer, among other seedlings, can be dug up to start a collection.

Carefully cut the soil with a sharp-edged knife, leaving enough space between the stem and the cut to enable a good ball of soil to come away with the seedling. Although some seedlings may be only a few inches above ground, they are often deep-rooted. The oak, for instance, has a deep root, although it may show only two or three inches of growth above ground. Avoid breaking off any more of the root than can possibly be helped, above the ball of soil. Trim broken roots with secateurs up to the ball of soil. Place the seedling immediately in a deep plastic bag, making sure that the soil

A red blossom peach, with a white blossom branch grafted on; also see the book jacket

A selection of Japanese and English containers

Top: Japanese white needle pine. *Bottom:* Willow ready for pruning

round the roots is damp. Cover with damp moss and pour a few drops of water in the bottom of the polythene bag to keep the inside humid. Tie the top of the bag.

For seedlings with smaller roots, cream and yoghurt tubs are handy containers. Metal milk-bottle holders will take about thirty tubs and are useful for transporting the seedlings. Now that dairies have started using plastic holders, they will often sell the metal ones for a few pence. The holders can be used in the car to prevent damage to the plant. Pot the seedlings in the soil from which they are growing, water well and leave until the following spring. Keep away from frost and cold winds. In March they can be re-potted into JI-1; a year later, start to cut the tap-root, re-pot and carry on pruning, pinching and training as for two-year-old trees.

Cuttings

Ripe wood as well as soft wood cuttings can be taken, providing the wood is not old. Select the cuttings for their leafiness. If the cuttings are to be taken when a deciduous tree is bare of leaf or in the dormant state, select the top growth of small trees or the tips of strong branches. Cuttings should be about three to four inches in length (conifers can be two and a half to three inches). Cut off three-quarters of the leaves and snip the others to half their size if they are more than an inch in diameter. This will reduce evaporation of moisture to a minimum.

Cut the end diagonally, just below a leaf node, then dip into a hormone rooting powder. The powder will stimulate root-growth. Plant in a plastic pot and water well with a sprinkler until water runs out of the bottom of the pot.

When a number of cuttings are required, dig a V-shaped

trench sheltered from the wind and line the bottom well with peat and sand. Prepare the cuttings, then lean them against the side of the trench, fill in and firm the soil by treading. These cuttings can be a couple of inches longer than for pots, but should be prepared in the same way.

Another method of striking cuttings is to prepare them as before and then mould a ball of clay (about an inch in diameter) round the cut stem. Plant in JI-1 compost in a plastic pot and water well. Plastic pots are useful for cuttings, since they do not dry out as quickly as clay pots. At all times, the cuttings must be kept moist but not soggy. A soggy compost will probably cause the stem to go soft and rot.

Grafting, Layering and Aerial Layering

Grafting is a useful remedy for mis-shapen trees, particularly trees that bear blossom. A well-grown tree, or one that has had a dead branch cut out, will sometimes balance better with another branch. If you have a tree of the same species that could do with one branch less, cut the branch out and graft it on to the tree that requires an extra branch. Badly-shaped dwarf trees can be kept in a healthy condition purely for this purpose. Alternatively, a branch of suitable size can be grafted from a parent tree.

In the spring select a branch, from either a miniature or the parent tree, with leaves right along the stem. Cut the end diagonally about one and a half inches, taking the point up on the opposite side a quarter of an inch; then make a diagonal cut in the trunk of the tree (about one-third the diameter of the trunk and as near the base as possible) at a point where the branch will balance. Fix the wedge-shaped end of the branch into the cut on the trunk and bind tightly with raffia, covering the whole of the cut. Keep under cover during the winter. When the graft has taken, re-pot the tree in JI-1. Untie the raffia a few weeks after re-potting. The following spring, re-pot into JI-2 or final compost.

Layering. This method is rather more limited, since not all trees have suitably low branches. In the spring select a low branch which is supple enough to bend until the centre, or thereabouts, touches the ground, making a curve. On the underside of the curve cut the cambium or outer layers

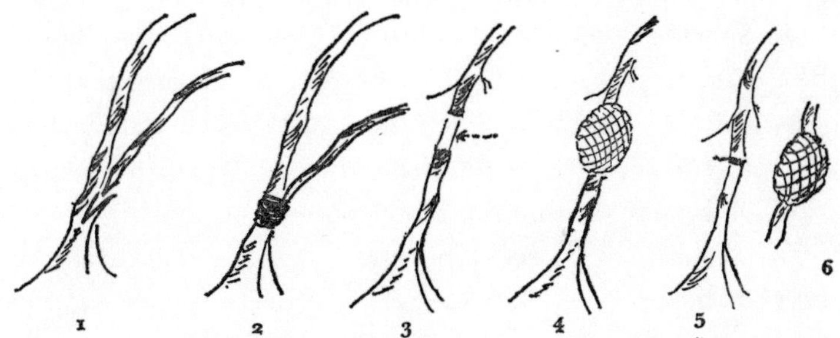

Fig. 17. *Replacing branches and aerial layering*: 1 Adding another branch can be done by grafting. Here the end of the branch is ready to be pushed into cut; 2 Bound with raffia; 3 Shows bark peeled back, ready to be covered; 4 Sphagnum moss covering the peeled bark and tied in place; 5 For smooth bark trees wire is bound tightly around the trunk; 6 It is then covered with sphagnum moss and tied

about one-third in. Peg down into the soil, or bury a pot and fill with sand, peat and soil. Make sure that the ground and pot are kept damp (pots can dry out quickly during a warm spell). When the layer has rooted, sever from the branch attached to the tree. If it has rooted from a pot, let it settle down for a few weeks before potting into JI-1. For branches rooted in the ground pot into their own soil until the following spring and then pot into JI-1. A year later, pot into JI-2 or final compost.

Aerial layering. Although this method may take a little longer, it is interesting because it enables you to choose right from the start the form that you wish your tree to take. It also produces a mature tree long before the method of growing from seed or seedlings.

Select a branch on a fully-grown tree or on an overgrown and healthy miniature with a good formation. At the place where you wish the root to form, peel back the bark about an inch all round. Make a ball of Sphagnum moss at least three times as thick as the branch, place it over and round the peeled branch, and bind with cord. Make sure that the moss is always damp right through. Wet it well and squeeze out before applying to the branch; then cover with a piece of plastic to keep in the humidity.

For smooth-bark trees, bind tightly with non-rust wire at the chosen part of the branch which is to root, then wrap in Sphagnum moss three times as thick as the diameter of the branch. The wire will cut into the branch, allowing roots to grow.

When sufficient roots have grown, saw off the branch below the root system and plant into a pot of JI-1. If the moss is difficult to remove, be careful not to force it away or you may break the roots. Take off any loose moss, leaving the rest until the next potting.

The chances of failure are less if the cutting of the branch is done in two operations. Saw through half the branch one week and the other half a couple of weeks later. Support the tree in the container, making sure that it is not exposed to strong sunlight. Shade with hessian or sacking. Transplant into JI-1 when free and into JI-2 or final compost the year after. Gradually expose the tree to the sunlight; by the spring it will be ready for pruning (a few weeks after re-potting).

Mature Trees

Training a small mature tree can be interesting, once you have had experience of training bonsai trees. Mature trees have the added advantage of looking well-advanced within a couple of years. Nurseries often have trees or shrubs that have not grown to expectation, either in height or in limb (this does not mean that the tree or shrub is not healthy). See that the tree has a good green head with ripe wood. Oddly-shaped trees are useful, but unhealthy, weakly trees are not and will give disappointing results. Neither should the tree have too many large branches which will need cutting out, although some branch cutting will most likely be needed, providing the branches are young enough to heal quickly. Seal all scars as soon as branches are cut off. Keep the tree in its pot until the following spring, when it can be re-potted and root-trained; at the same time, cut back half the tap-root and then cut the rest the following spring. Each month, throughout the late spring and summer, pinch out the tips and unwanted growth and prune branches where necessary. Take a good look at the shape of the tree and decide what is to be left in, gradually taking away unwanted growth. In the second year, pot into final compost.

Digging up Mature Trees

An opportunity may come along to dig up small trees. Although these may be stunted, perhaps by wind conditions or by overcrowding, they will make ideal bonsai trees as long as they are healthy. First you will need some good muscles, as some small trees are quite hefty. Have your polythene bag with damp moss handy, and also raffia and sacking.

With a sharp-edged tool push and cut the soil in a circle, a foot from the tree trunk. Working away from the trunk, dig a trench until the tree is standing on an island. With the long-pronged fork dig well under the island, keeping as many roots intact as possible. You will not doubt have to break off some of the deep roots – providing there are plenty in the ball it will not matter. Spread out the sacking nearby. Turn the tree on its side and trim the broken root; then, lifting from the bottom, place it on the sack. Lift up the edges of the sacking all round and tie it like a parcel. Soak it well with water before placing it in the moist moss in the polythene bag.

When you arrive home, dig a hole large enough to take the ball of soil comfortably, not burying the roots any deeper than before, and leave the tree until next spring.

In the meantime, take a good look at the shape so that you can decide which branches are to come out and what shape the tree will most easily assume. Although branches will require training, it is better with older trees to keep as near as possible to the shape in which it has grown. Providing the tree looks healthy, it can be dug up, root-pruned and re-potted in the following spring. Cut the tap-root back and prune the long fibrous roots. Pot into a container filled partly with its own soil and partly with final compost. Start leaf pruning and pinching out. Cut out no more than two branches at intervals this year, but remove all unwanted branchlets. The following year, re-pot into final compost and cut out another two branches if necessary. Continue leaf pruning and pinching out. After this, the tree should be treated as a mature tree. It may be necessary to re-pot a little more often until the roots have formed the required ball.

WARNING: Do not grub up plants without first asking permission of the owner of the land. On common land pulling up plants is forbidden. A great deal of damage is being done by the ruthless grubbing up of plants. However careful you are, you can be the unlucky one who is caught! The penalties are heavy.

Buying Mature Trees

When buying grown trees, do not buy a 'pig in a poke'! Go to a reputable grower and see the tree for yourself. Trees up to ten years old usually cost, in Britain, roughly £1 to £1.50 per year of life. A five-year-old trained tree will cost about £5 to £7.50. After ten years old, prices depend on the species and how well the tree has been trained. A fifty-year-old tree can be worth hundreds of pounds. I have known older trees change hands for thousands of pounds. In the United States and elsewhere prices depend on location and availability – but fine bonsai trees are never cheap!

Most growers will provide a feeding and training chart. However, by following the method described in this book you should be able to keep the tree healthy.

Joining a bonsai club can be very helpful. There is no need for the club to be local, as quarterly newsletters are sent out to each member. Clubs also give free advice. One club I know of will look after members' trees when they are away from home (free of charge). A discount is also given on trees bought from the club – The Bonsai Club, St Mary's Gardens, Worplesdon, Surrey. The annual subscription of £1.25 is certainly good value.

CHAPTER ELEVEN

MAKING A START

Various ways of growing from suitable plants are listed in this chapter. There are many other trees that make good bonsai (a more comprehensive list of suitable trees will be found at the end of the book). The trees listed in the sections that follow are among those which, on the whole, respond well to the growing method described.

Seeds and Pips

Growing from seeds and pips is, perhaps, the easiest method for the beginner, since training right from the start will give a good insight into the needs of the trees. Shaping the more supple branches is helpful at first, until the fingers become adept in training stiffer and harder branches. Start seeds and pips in JI-seedling in seed-pans, during the appropriate season mentioned below. Botanical names of trees are given in brackets:

Apples – most types – avoid cookers: Pip – Autumn
Berberis – nearly all species: Seed – when ripe
Cedar (*Cedrus*): Seed – when ripe
Common Hornbeam (*Carpinus*): Seed – Autumn
Ash (*Fraxinus*): Seed – when green, or stratify when brown
Plane (*Platanus*), British hybrid species: Seed borne from British trees
Elder (*Sambucus*): Seed

Lime or Linden (*Tilia*): Seed – may take up to two years to germinate

Rowan (*Sorbus*), popularly known as Mountain Ash to which it bears no relation, belonging to the apple and pear family:

Seed – may take up to two years to germinate

Pears – as for apple: Pip

Hawthorn (*Crataegus*): Seeds – stratified in sand when ripe

Yew (*Taxus*): Seed – in March

Holly (*Ilex*): Stratify berry in Autumn, sow in Spring

Citrus fruits: Orange, tangerine, lemon, grapefruit: Pips – when at their best in late Autumn or early Spring.

Nuts

Other forms of seeds are the various nuts: in particular chestnut, hazel and acorn. Horse chestnut germinates quickly. Acorn is a slow grower once it has germinated. Spanish chestnut is often slower in growth and more difficult to germinate than horse chestnut.

Horse chestnut (*Aesculus*): Nut – plant when ripe, late Autumn

Spanish chestnut (*Castanea*): Nut – plant Autumn

Hazel (*Corylus*): Nut – plant Autumn

Walnut (*Juglans*): Nut – plant when ripe, late Autumn

Oak (*Quercus*): Acorn – as soon as fallen in Autumn

Fruit Stones

Stratification of fruit stones will be necessary in most cases. Place the stones in pots or pans filled with sand, cover with several inches and plunge in the open ground. Leave through the winter and plant in spring. There are 400 species of cherry (*Prunus*) to choose from. Keep well protected until mature, placing outside only in the summer. During the winter keep in temperatures above freezing-point, even when mature:

Cherry (*Prunus*): Stone – plant in spring after stratifying

Peach (*Prunus persica*): Stone – plant in spring (some require stratifying)

Nectarine, natural sport of the peach: As for peach

Plum: Will grow without stratifying

Damson: As for plum

Seedlings

All seedlings should be dug up with a ball of soil.

Crab Apple (*Malus*). Better than seeds: Plant Autumn

Rowan (*Sorbus*): Autumn or winter

Willow (*Salix*): Autumn or winter

Alder (*Alnus*): Spring

Horse Chestnut (*Aesculus*): Spring

Maple Sycamore (*Acer*): Spring

Spanish Chestnut (*Castanea*). Better than seeds: Spring

Hazel (*Corylus*): October

Beech (*Fagus*): Spring

Oak (*Quercus*): April to May, September to October

Plane (*Platanus*): October to March

Hornbeam (*Carpinus*): October to March

Poplar (*Populus*): October to February

Pear (*Pyrus*): Late Autumn and Winter

Elder (*Sambucus*): Autumn

Lime (*Tilia*): October to March

Larch (*Larix*): Autumn

Yew (*Taxus*): September

Juniper (*Juniperus*): September to October, or March

Spruce (*Picea*) – all species: Spring and Autumn
Chaenomeles (often known as quince): Spring

Cuttings

Plant cuttings in JI-1 and keep under glass until rooted. Cover with newspaper during frosty weather, removing it in the morning.

Alder (*Alnus*): Cutting after leaf-fall
Crab Apple (*Malus*): dormant wood
Plane (*Platanus*): October to March
Holly (*Ilex*): Spring, half-ripe wood
Poplar (*Populus*): dormant wood
Elder (*Sambucus*): hard wood Autumn
Yew (*Taxus*): September
Box (*Buxus*): August to September
Juniper (*Juniperus*): Late Summer

Grafting

There are very few trees that cannot be grafted. The trees listed below should graft easily and are ideal for those who have not tried their hand at grafting. All grafting should be done in the spring.

Crab Apple (*Malus*)
Cherry (*Prunus*)
Rowan (*Sorbus*)
Horse Chestnut (*Aesculus*)
Hazel (*Corylus*)
Beech (*Fagus*)
Hornbeam (*Carpinus*)
Pear (*Pyrus*)
Hawthorn (*Crataegus*)

Nearly all varieties of *Prunus* will graft, as will most flower-bearing trees and conifers.

Aerial Layering

Aerial layering should take place in late spring or early June.

Maple (*Acer*)
Elm (*Ulmus*)
Holly (*Ilex*)
Spruce (*Picea*)

Layering Low Branches

Three of the easiest trees to layer:

Azalea – Japanese
Spruce (*Picea*)
Chaenomeles

CHAPTER TWELVE

FLOWERING PLANTS

There are a few flowering garden plants that can be trained by bonsai methods to show their flowers to the best advantage. Chrysanthemums are used a great deal by Japanese growers and make delightfully showy plants. The best species is known

Fig. 18. *Cascade chrysanthemum.* Allow the roots to grow long enough to straddle the rocks, with the tips in the compost. Keep more of the flower buds than for blossoming trees. Three side shoots have been left – flowers come from the secondary shoots.

as 'Cascade' and has a small flower. As its name implies, it makes a good cascade style. These plants can be trained to grow in oblique, upright or cascading shapes. They can also be grown against pieces of tree-trunks or over rocks. Whichever style is chosen, they make a beautiful picture as they form a mass of flowers in late summer.

To achieve a Cascade style, tie three or four lengths of raffia or cord under the pot, bring it through the pot hole and up over the side, and anchor to a heavy stone or something solid which will not easily move about. Tie at intervals to the stone, taking care to space the cord. Plant the seedling

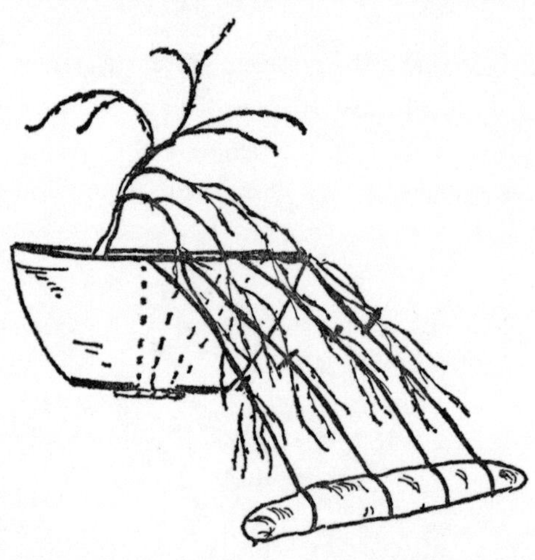

Fig. 19. *Cascade training flowering plants.* Tie raffia or cord to a label under the container before re-potting. Bring the ties through the pot and over the side and tie to a heavy stone. Anchor the main stems of the plant to the ties

and, when the stems are long enough, tie each one to the cord or raffia.

Pinch out unwanted growth and buds, leaving a central bud to each spray. Leave more buds for flowering than for trees with blossom in order to obtain a display effect. On the other hand, it is unwise to overcrowd the stem, for this will weaken the branch. In the second year the cord can be cut away and the cascade should now stay in position.

For the *Chokkan* or upright style, allow the plant to attain the height required in the first year, stopping regularly from May to September to induce a good branch or two. Improve the shape in the second year by pinching unwanted growth.

For all these styles, after flowering you should cut back the shoot to a second leaf and feed with liquid manure (the stated dose for garden plants). Apply fresh compost each spring. When taking the plant out of the container, leave a ball of soil on the roots, trimming any roots that come through the ball.

Older branches (not shoots) should be cut out, the new shoots from the stem replacing them. On older plants remove all basal shoots (shoots low on the stem).

Flowering garden plants can be used for bonsai providing they have a strong or woody stem. On the whole, they will not last as long as the trees; but, when properly grown and trained, they will give several years of enjoyment. They grow much more quickly than the trees, often giving a display of colour in the second year.

The Michaelmas daisy is another flowering plant that can be grown by the bonsai method in the same way as the chrysanthemum. Make sure that you grow the treated daisies, as they are prone to mildew.

Rosemary and lavender both make delightful plants. Both are seen at their best in the *Chokkan* style, which allows the flowers to show off. Wild roses are ideal and can be grown in any style. They need pruning after flowering. If you grow roses in a Cascade style, cut out the old wood after flowering and tie the new shoots to the cord. For upright styles the old wood will need to be cut out and pruned in March. Otherwise, wild roses can be treated in the same way as the Cascade chrysanthemum.

CHAPTER THIRTEEN

MAME BONSAI

There are certain differences in the training of the *Mame* (mah-may) bonsai, which is a miniature of a miniature. Some of these tiny trees are no more than an inch or two high. The advantage of *Mame* trees is that they are ready for display much earlier than the larger bonsai. They are ideal to grow where there is a lack of garden space. They can be displayed in small flats and on balconies, providing they will have some sun and fresh air. They can be grown in individual containers – several containers placed together make an interesting display on a glass shelf.

Choose the simple styles for *Mame* trees – Cascade, oblique and upright. The size of the pots range from an inch or two to about six inches. It must be remembered that these tiny pots soon dry out and will need careful attention to prevent the plant from shrivelling up.

Sowing From Seed

This is probably the best method for the beginner, as the tiny plant is easier to control. Sow the seed straight into the container. Use fresh seed or sow immediately after stratifying. Sieve the compost to make a fine tilth and then add sieved clay to the soil (about a quarter part). This will help to keep the compost moist and bind it a little so that the tree does not topple over as it grows.

Sow the seed with a light covering of compost and sprinkle

Chinese elm, seven years old

Viburnum

Pyracantha

Cotoneaster

a little sand over the top. Moisten by placing the container in water up to the rim. Cover with glass or thick polythene, which should be removed as soon as the seedling shows above the compost.

Seeds sown in a number of containers make an excellent window-box display. Alternatively, half a dozen sown in a dish make a 'forest' of trees. In any case, it is as well to grow a number of *Mame*, as weakly seedlings are useless and should be discarded. Those that have grown too large or have oversize leaves should also be discarded.

Root pruning takes place in March, as with the larger bonsai. Cut the tap-root in stages over three years, unless the growth is particularly vigorous, in which case the tap-root should be cut in two seasons. When re-potting, make the compost slightly bulkier by sieving it through a coarser mesh (this will give the roots a better grip and prevent the tree from leaning over). Leaf and branch pruning starts immediately after the first re-potting. In April, cut the growth back quite hard to a bud. Pinch out, leaf cut and cut out unwanted branchlets right through the summer.

Wire training is not difficult if done just before the shoots break. Pot the trees in February and wire train in early March. Usually one season is enough to train the trunk into shape. Branches may require further training at a later stage. Take all wire off before placing the tree in its winter quarters.

Spray the tree regularly during warm weather. With an occasional dunking, spraying is often sufficient to keep the tiny containers moist. If kept slightly dry rather than over-damp, the trees will require less pinching and pruning once they have matured. Keep the trees in filtered sun during the spring and summer. Allow them to catch gentle rain, but beware of heavy thundery showers in the summer. Place under top cover during prolonged rain.

Mame trees must be cut back hard each year. When cutting, try not to make the tree look too stark. Allow the leader or main trunk to grow a little taller than the intended height, then cut the top a little below the height required. From the commencement of cutting continue in this way with the main stem, and branches will thicken, particularly the spreading branches on the upright and oblique styles.

When a seedling has little in the way of branches, cut the

Fig. 20. *Mame*. Three tiny *Mame* bonsai. The Scots pine on the right is still in training; the two lower branches will be cut out to give the tree maturity by thickening the trunk. The other two are trained to shape, only requiring pinching out of leaves and of any new shoots that may appear

top off the head and cut out any side-growth at the end of April. This will encourage the denuded trunk to shoot branches.

Cuttings

Cuttings should be three inches long, with three leaves left at the top. Plant in shallow trays in JI-1. When growth has started, keep only the best shoots, discarding the others. Pot up in autumn and a couple of weeks later wire train the trunk. In the summer, pinch and prune leaves and branchlets as for seeds. Leave outside during warm weather. Potting and wiring in the autumn give the plant a chance to recover before growth begins.

Woodland Trees

One often finds tiny woody-stemmed trees, about as large as seedlings, growing in woods and copses. These are usually seedlings retarded – although basically healthy – through adverse conditions such as overcrowding, roots stunted by thick growth or other setbacks. They are worth digging up to start a collection. Dig them up with a ball of soil as described in Chapter 10. Then plant them in the garden or in a window-box until the following spring. In the spring dig them up carefully and trim the roots. Place the plants in containers and slightly bulky compost consisting of a quarter part leafmould, sand and clay mixed with JI-1. Two to three weeks later, when the tree has settled and is firm, start wire training the trunk and branches. Pinch and cut out unwanted growth through the summer, as for seeds.

The following plants make good *Mame* bonsai :

Azalea : Cuttings – lime-free compost
Acer (Maple) : Cuttings or seedlings
Juniperus : Cuttings or seeds
Tamarix : Cuttings – may need layering
Picea : Cuttings or seeds
Pinus : Seedlings
Berberis : Cuttings or seeds
Cotoneaster : Cuttings, seedlings or seeds
Ilex (Holly) : Seedlings, cuttings or seeds from berries.

CHAPTER FOURTEEN

EDUCATION AND THERAPEUTICS

Education

Educating children to appreciate nature is essential if we are to preserve the art of growing plants in this age of steel and concrete. Growing miniature trees as part of nature study in schools would give pupils an interest in the parent plant and would also prove popular in itself, particularly if the trees are grown from nuts such as the acorn and chestnut. As pupils progress to higher forms, it should not be difficult for them to continue training and tending the tree until they leave school, when it will have reached a mature state.

With Britain joining the Common Market, there will be a need for many specialized commodities for export to Europe. In this country horticulture has now become a profession based on the best scientific knowledge. Already, some of the finest roses are grown in Britain and many other British plants are beginning to spread across the world.

The time is rapidly approaching when growers will require a diploma to grow commercially. For young people leaving school at sixteen who are interested in horticulture, there is a scheme administered by the Agriculture, Horticulture and Forestry Training Board, covering a three-year course in the basic training of fruit-growing, nursery and glasshouse holdings, and market gardening. The Local Government Parks

Departments also have apprenticeship schemes for practical horticulture ranging from three to five years. The last two of the five years are devoted to specialized subjects.

Sandwich courses beginning after one year's basic training prepare students for the Ordinary National Diploma in Commercial Horticulture.

After three years' basic training, most of the Botanical Gardens will accept students between the ages of nineteen and twenty-one to further their tuition. Some require specialized subjects. Nearly all include lectures, demonstrations and practical work in their curriculum. These courses can lead to a Diploma.

A sandwich course in Biological Science can lead to an Honours Degree and Teachers' Training Courses are also available for students who have the necessary qualifications.

Courses up to the Diploma standard will be of immense value when specializing in any one subject, including the growing of bonsai trees.

At the present time Japan produces the best miniature trees, exporting mature, partly trained trees for continued training. Even so, not all trees grown in Japan are allowed to come to Britain or to many of the Common Market countries, owing to disease. With the increasing interest in bonsai trees there is a wide open market for new growers.

Therapeutics

Growing miniature trees has its uses in therapeutic medicine. Invalids, elderly people and children requiring therapy would not only find an interest in growing these tiny trees, but would be able to broaden their knowledge by studying books written about the parent plants and growth.

People with disabilities, especially those confined to wheel chairs, would find growing bonsai trees a delightful hobby.

Where there is a garden available, a raised bed can be built on which to stand the trees. A reading or bed table laid across the chair makes a useful bench to work on. Many new tools are coming on the market for wheel-chair gardeners, including long-handled pincers which have wide blades to reach pots out of range.

Where there is no garden, a bench or table placed in a cool, light room can be used for standing the trees. In the summer they will need to be placed outside on the window-ledge or on a balcony, to keep them healthy and to enable the sun to ripen the wood.

There are untold possibilities in the art of growing bonsai trees, either in schools, commercially, for therapeutic purposes, or simply for the pleasure of growing them as a hobby.

Appendix

LIST OF TREES AND SHRUBS SUITABLE FOR BONSAI

(Note: FC Final compost)

Tree	*Origin*	*Soil for Mature Trees*
Alder (*Alnus glutinosa*)	Native	F C
Apple	Native	F C
Apple, Crab (*Malus sylvestris*)	Native	F C
Ash (*Fraxinus excelsior*)	Native	F C – pinch of lime
Aspen (*Populus tremula*)	Native	F C – pinch of lime
Azalea	Japanese	No lime – compost
Beech (*Fagus sylvatica*)	Native	F C – pinch of lime
Berberis (*B. darwinii*)	S. America	F C
Birch (*Betula* species)	Native	F C
Box (*Buxus suffruticosa*)	Native	F C
B. vulgaris	Native	F C
Buckthorn (*Rhamnus cathartica*)	Native	F C
Chestnut, Sweet (*Castanea sativa*)	Roman Occupation	F C
Chestnut, Horse (*Aesculus hippocastanum*)	16th century	F C
Cedar (*Cedrus libani*)	Lebanon	F C
C. atlantica	N. Africa	F C
C. deodora	Himalayan Mountains	F C
Cotoneaster	Europe, W. Africa, Asia	F C
Cypress, Common (*Cupressus sempervirens*)	18th century	F C
Cypress, False (*Chamaecyparis lawsoniana*)	Recent years from N. America	F C
C. nootkatensis	Found in Welshpool	F C
Dogwood (*Cornus sanguinea*)	Native	F C
Elder (*Sambucus nigra*)	Native	F C – moist

Elm, English (*Ulmus procera*)	Native	F C
Fir, Douglas (*Pseudotsuga menziesii*)	Native for several hundred years	F C
Hawthorn (*Crataegus* species)	Native	F C
Hazel (*Corylus avellana*)	Native	F C – extra sand
Holly (*Ilex*)	Native	F C
Hornbeam (*Carpinus betulus*)	Native	F C
Jasmine, Winter (*Jasminum nudiflorum*)	Britain – 16th century	F C
Juniper (*Juniperus*)	Northern Hemisphere	F C
Larch (*Larix* species)	Europe	F C
Lime or Linden (*Tilia*)		
T. platyphyllos – small-leaved		
T. cordata – common	Europe	F C – pinch of lime
T. vulgaris – hybrid of above		
Maple (*Acer*)		
A. campestre – field maple	Native	F C – pinch of lime
A. platanoides – Norway maple	Est. 17th century	F C – pinch of lime
A. pseudoplatanus – sycamore	Est. 16th century	F C – pinch of lime
Oak (*Quercus*)		
Q. cerris – Turkey oak	18th century	F C
Q. robur, Q. petraea	Native	F C
Pear	Native	F C
Pear, Wild (*Pyrus communis*)	Probably Native	F C
Pine (*Pinus sylvestris*) – Scots Pine	Native	F C
P. pinaster – Maritime Pine	Europe	F C
Plane (*Platanus acerifolia*)	From warmer regions	F C
P. occidentalis	N. America 200 years	F C
P. orientalis	S.E. Europe 400 years	F C
Poplar (*Populus nigra* var. *pyramidalis*) – Lombardy popular	Italy, est. 18th century	F C
P. alba (white)	Native	F C
P. canescens (grey)	Native	F C – moist
Privet (*Ligustrum*)	Native	F C
Prunus – genus of deciduous trees including almond, apricot, cherry, nectarine, peach, plum, damson	Many from Japan	F C

PYRACANTHA	Mostly from China	F C
QUINCE (*Chaenomeles*)	N. Asia	F C
ROWAN (*Sorbus aucuparia*)	Native	F C
Often called Mountain Ash but no relation to the ash	Native	F C
ROSE, GUELDER (*Viburnum opulus*)	Native	F C
ROSE, WILD (*Rosa arvensis and R. canina*)	Native	F C
SLOE OR BLACKTHORN (*Prunus spinosa*)	Native	F C
VIBURNUM	British Way-faring tree	F C
WALNUT (*Juglans regia*)	Asia	F C
WELLINGTONIA (*Sequoiadendron giganteum*)	Est. 19th century	F C
WHITETHORN (*Crataegus*) – May tree	See Hawthorn	
WILLOW (*Salix alba*) – White willow	Native	F C – moist
S. caprea – Goat or common sallow	Native	F C – moist
S. babylonica – Weeping willow	Asia	F C – moist
S. fragilis – Crack willow	Northern Britain	F C – moist
S. pentandra – Bay-leaved Willow	Northern England	F C – moist
YEW (*Taxus baccata*)	Native	F C

Index

Bold figures denote illustrations